TABLE OF CONTENTS

INTRODUCTION
LEADERSHIP
CONCEPTS OF LEADERSHIP
  FACTORS OF LEADERSHIP
WAYS OF DEFINING LEADERSHIP
A STAND
LEADERS ALWAYS CELEBRATE SMALL WINS
  Reasons Why Leaders Should Celebrate Wins
GREAT LEADERS TAKE THE BLAME AND PASS ON THE CREDIT
A GOOD LEADER
  5 Common Traits Of Great Leadership
IMPORTANCE OF LEADERSHIP FOR ORGANIZATION
CONCLUSION

INTRODUCTION

A simple definition is that leadership is the art of motivating a group of people to act towards achieving a common goal. In other words, if you inspire anyone to do anything then you are a leader. In a business setting, this can mean directing workers and colleagues with a strategy to meet the company's needs.

This leadership captures the essentials of being able to inspire others and being prepared to do so. Effective leadership is based upon ideas (whether original or borrowed, remember the wheel was only invented once), but won't happen unless those ideas can be communicated to others in a way that engages them enough to act in a direcection that is best for the group as a whole.

Put even more simply, the leader is the inspiration and director of the action. He or she is the person in the group that possesses the combination of personality and leadership skills that makes others want to follow his or her direction.

As a generalization, Leadership is the most essential ability that makes organizations successful. The faculty to have regions, districts, and departments follow a vision is sought after by many but owned by few. Your most prominent organizations have large groups with varied talents, cooperate and perform due to influence. Leadership is as much of an institution as it is an individual; we not only follow people, we follow purpose. When there is structure, strategy, and an established culture it is easier to buy-in and execute. Often times, employees never meet or get to know Executive Leadership but function because of Organizational Design.

In this book you will learn the foundation of being a good leader. This book will, in no way, give you all of the tools you will need. Any good leader will tell you, they never stop learning, never stop growing, and never stop trying to be a better leader.

LEADERSHIP

Some view leadership as a series of specific traits or characteristics. Others see it as comprised of certain skills and knowledge. And some, me included, think of leadership as a process. This view of leadership, as a process, places an emphasis on social interaction and relationship. This is the idea that leadership is a type of relationship, one that typically includes influencing others in a certain direction. This leads to my current working definition of leadership: Leadership is a relationship that involves the mobilizing, influencing, and guiding of others toward desired goals. This definition does not assume that the goals are shared or even explicit. The word desire simply means that someone in the relationship, perhaps just the person in a leadership role, wants a particular outcome. The following are some definitions that have a bias toward leadership as a process:

"Leadership is a process of giving purpose (meaningful direction) to collective effort, and causing willing effort to be expended to achieve purpose." (Jacobs & Jaques)

"Leadership is the process of influencing the activities of an individual or a group in efforts toward goal achievement in a given situation." (Hersey & Blanchard)

"Leadership is an attempt at influencing the activities of followers through the communication process and toward the attainment of some goal or goals." (Donelly)

"Leadership is defined as the process of influencing the activities of an organized group toward goal achievement." (Rauch & Behling)

"Leadership is interpersonal influence, exercised in a situation, and directed, through the communication process, toward the attainment of a specified goal or goals." (Tannenbaum, et al)

It has been my experience that many organizational leaders, knowingly or unknowingly, view leadership as a set of specific traits or skills. Below are a few definitions that are grounded in skills and, to a lesser extent, traits.

"Leadership is a function of knowing yourself, having a vision that is well communicated, building trust among colleagues, and taking effective action to realize your own leadership potential". (Bennis)

"Leadership is about articulating visions, embodying values, and creating the environment within which things can be accomplished." (Richards and Engle)

"Leadership is the creation of a vision about a desired future state which seeks to enmesh all members of an organization in its net." (Bryman)

"It is a complex moral relationship between people, based on trust, obligation, commitment, emotion, and a shared vision of the good." (Ciulla)

These definitions are entirely valid perspectives — they are simply different from a leadership as process perspective. Having said that, it is my impression that, overall, definitions of leadership are becoming more process and relationship oriented.

How Important Is It to Have a Definition of Leadership?

In my role as a leadership consultant it is not necessary for me to share my clients definition of leadership – but it is important to know whether they have a definition and, if they do, what is included in that definition. If there isn't an understanding of what leadership entails it diminishes the likelihood that the client will get what they want from our relationship. It is similar to a client looking to hire a consultant to increase employee engagement and, after digging a bit deeper with the client, discovering that what they are actually looking for is a way to improve the efficiency of work processes. A leader sets the end point and if we don't know where we want to go then we don't know the path to get there.

Is Leading Different than Managing? (Pros and Cons)

Management and Leadership are two very different systems of human behavior. Both are essential to the success of an organization; yet, like the repulsing polarity of two magnets, they push against one another and, if not kept in balance, can end up ejecting one or the other causing great damage to the organization and its people. It is difficult, yet necessary, to maintain both strong leadership and strong management simultaneously.

People are naturally reluctant to step into change and the discomfort we experience when we find ourselves in the midst of ambiguity. Much of what we call "organization" is the struggle to reign in that ambiguity and bring things back to a state of equilibrium. Management is about developing systems and processes that enable us to take dominion over chaos. It is an attempt to create a semblance of order and constancy in an inherently complex situation. It's about designing plans and systems for monitoring progress and controlling outcomes. It involves solving problems, giving reports, having meetings, and developing policies, all for the purpose of bringing things to a place of efficiency, where the ambiguity is dispelled and people can feel comfortable again.

The problem is that, in a rapidly-changing environment, equilibrium can be deadly. The external environment today is a bit like whitewater rafting. To survive, you have to constantly shift your weight from one side of the raft to the other, thrust your paddle first to the left and then to the right, or use it to push off a rapidly approaching rock. This is when you need leadership rather than management.

Leadership is about change. It's about helping the organization define its vision, one that can take advantage of opportunities and avoid oncoming threats. It's about challenging people to grow and to unleash their yet untapped potential. It's about inspiring people to step into uncharted territory. Leaders get nervous when things are running too smoothly; often introducing innovative ideas just to stir things up a bit. Whereas managers constantly try to adjust to change, leaders are in the business of producing change.

It's important to understand that both are necessary for success. Unfortunately, some organizations I have been acquainted with continue to value management over leadership. In these situations, the leadership function can be mistakenly identified as subversive to the organization's welfare. The call for unity is often a demand that those with innovative thoughts keep them to themselves. The status quo is confused with the sacred. If organizations are to stay afloat and thrive in today's volatile environment, they must recognize that leadership is essential. In the Bible there is a saying about putting new wine into old wineskins and thus causing the wineskins to burst because they lack flexibility. The new wine must be put into new wineskins. Management tries to hold the wine in a manageable form. Leadership is the process of changing from the old, dried-out, leaky wineskins to the new, more resilient, more adjustable forms. Another way to look at Leadership vs. Management is: Managers make sure the job gets done, Leaders make sure the goals are achieved.

View That Separating "Leading" from "Managing" Can Be Destructive

Another view is that to be a very effective member of an organization (whether executive, middle manager, or entry-level worker), you need skills in the functions of planning, organizing, leading and coordinating activities -- the key is you need to be able to emphasize different skills at different times.

Yes, leading is different than planning, organizing and coordinating because leading is focused on influencing people, while the other functions are focused on "resources" in addition to people. But that difference is not enough to claim that "leading is different than managing" any more than one can claim that "planning is different than managing" or "organizing is different than managing".

The assertion that "leading is different than managing" -- and the ways that these assertions are made -- can cultivate the view that the activities of planning, organizing and coordinating are somehow less important than leading. The assertion can also convince others that they are grand and gifted leaders who can ignore the mere activities of planning, organizing and coordinating -- they can leave these lesser activities to others with less important things to do in the organization. This view can leave carnage in organizations.

Your position as leader does not take work away from you. To the contrary, being a leader means you take on the responsibility for making sure the work is done and done in a way that furthers the goals and desires of the team. All to often people think that once they do the hard work of climing the leadership ladder they can relax and enjoy the spoils of leadership. This is a fast track to failure. When you become a leader your you may not be responable for the day to day operation of a certain duty but you must realize that, even though you don't preform the job anymore your responsibility for making sure that job is done, and done correctly, increases. If a mistake happens it will ultimately be you that those above you call to correct the problem and to place the blame.

Additional Perspectives on Theories of Leadership

As you continue your study on leadership you will find that you are using many different "styles" of leadership. It is important to understand some of those "styles" and to start thinking about how they would be incorporated into different situations. While you may have a "default" style that you like you will most likely use many different styles over your carreer.

Behavioral Theory

This theory focuses especially on what highly effective leaders do. This theory is often preferred by educators because behaviors can rather easily be seen and duplicated. The major criticisms are that it doesn't help leaders know when to use certain behaviors and to share their motives for using those behaviors.

Contingency Theory

This theory states that a leader's effectiveness is contingent on how well the leader's style matches a specific setting or situation. And how, you may ask, is this different from situational theory? In situational the focus is on adapting to the situation, whereas contingency states that effective leadership depends on the degree of fit between a leader's qualities and style and that of a specific situation or context.

Functional Theory

This theory focuses especially on the behaviors needed to help a group to improve its effectiveness and achieve its goals. The theory identifies the specific functions needed by leadership for addressing certain situations. Another way to think of this theory is, you place people where they are needed the most.

Great Man Theory

This theory focuses on the traits and actions of those who are considered to be great leaders, as if they were born with those traits of leadership -- that leadership is a trait of those people, more than any skills that they had learned.

Path-Goal Theory

This theory is about how leaders motivate followers to accomplish identified objectives. It postulates that effective leaders have the ability to improve the motivation of followers by clarifying the paths and removing obstacles to high performance and desired objectives. The underlying beliefs of path-goal theory (grounded in expectancy theory) are that people will be more focused and motivated if they believe they are capable of high performance, believe their effort will result in desired outcomes, and believe their work is worthwhile.

Servant Leadership Theory

This conceptualization of leadership reflects a philosophy that leaders should be servants first. It suggests that leaders must place the needs of followers, customers, and the community ahead of their own interests in order to be effective. The idea of servant leadership has a significant amount of popularity within leadership circles – but it is difficult to describe it as a theory inasmuch as a set of beliefs and values that leaders are encouraged to embrace.

Situational Theory

This theory suggests that different situations require different styles of leadership. That is, to be effective in leadership requires the ability to adapt or adjust one's style to the circumstances of the situation. The primary factors that determine how to adapt are an assessment of the competence and commitment of a leader's followers. The assessment of these factors determines if a leader should use a more directive or supportive style.

Skills Theory

This theory states that learned knowledge and acquired skills/abilities are significant factors in the practice of effective leadership. Skills theory by no means disavows the connection between inherited traits and the capacity to be an effective leader – it simply argues that learned skills, a developed style, and acquired knowledge, are the real keys to leadership performance. It is of course the belief that skills theory is true that warrants all the effort and resources devoted to leadership training and development.

Trait Theory

This theory postulates that people are either born or not born with the qualities that predispose them to success in leadership roles. That is, that certain inherited qualities, such as personality and cognitive ability, are what underlie effective leadership. There have been hundreds of studies to determine the most important leadership traits, and while there is always going to be some disagreement, intelligence, sociability, and drive (aka determination) are consistently cited as key qualities.

Transactional Theory

This is a theory that focuses on the exchanges that take place between leaders and followers. It is based in the notion that a leader's job is to create structures that make it abundantly clear what is expected of his/her followers and also the consequences (i.e. rewards and punishments) for meeting or not meeting these expectations. This theory is often likened to the concept and practice of management and continues to be an extremely common component of many leadership models and organizational structures.

Transformational Theory

This theory states that leadership is the process by which a person engages with others and is able to create a connection that results in increased motivation and morality in both followers and leaders. It is often likened to the theory of charismatic leadership that espouses that leaders with certain qualities, such as confidence, extroversion, and clearly stated values, are best able to motivate followers. The key in transformational leadership is for the leader to be attentive to the needs and motives of followers in an attempt to help them reach their maximum potential. In addition, transformational leadership typically describes how leaders can initiate, develop, and implement important changes in an organization. This theory is often discussed in contrast with transactional leadership.

Different Frameworks and Elements of Leadership

The following models usually have a suggested framework and/or set of elements to implement that model of leadership. However, some of the following models have also been mentioned as theories or styles. As with the different theories, an acquaintance with the different models can further your understanding of leadership

Adaptive Leadership

The adaptive leader needs to be able to connect organizational change to the core values, capabilities, and dreams of the relevant stakeholders. The adaptive leader seeks to foster a culture that collects and honors diversity of opinion and uses this collective knowledge for the good of the organization. The adaptive leader knows that change and learning can be painful for people, and is able to anticipate and counteract any reluctant behavior related to the pain. The adaptive leader understands that large scale change is an incremental process and that he/she needs to be persistent and willing to withstand pressure to take shortcuts.

Appreciative Leadership

Appreciative leadership asserts that we all never fully "arrive" ... instead, we all do the best we can a day at a time, using the best tools and resources that are available to us. Appreciative leadership shares generative stories and practical tools that can help each of us to feel that we belong and are valued, and to walk that path a little more consistently and consciously. In so doing, it may help others do the same – and make the world kinder, better place

Authentic Leadership

Authentic leadership asserts the need for leaders to be truly authentic human beings in their roles as leaders. Authenticity has a variety of interpretations in this approach, ranging from being respectfully honest and direct with others in the moment to be fully self-realized human beings. Critics assert that we must be careful about how we interpret authenticity so that we do not romanticize and idealize the concept to the extent that no human being could ever achieve that status - and thus the approach inadvertently becomes inauthentic in itself.

Dynamic Leadership

Dynamical leaders pay attention to three conditions to ensure an effective, highly functioning organization: coherence, resilience, and fitness. Coherence can be thought of as an interdependence of parts. Dynamic leaders are constantly scanning their environment for potential surprises, and regard blips and trends as pieces of a larger puzzle to be solved. Resilience is the ability to integrate, re-calibrate and recover quickly when challenged

Heroic Leadership

Heroic leadership is when followers are greatly influenced by a leader in whom they have strong confidence to solve complex problems and achieve great goals -- in that sense, the leader is their hero. Critics caution us to not take this to extremes, that is, that the hero is not to be seen as someone who can save us from any situation. Rather, the heroic leader is someone that we greatly respect and, thus, we are willing to follow him or her.

Systems and Complexity Leadership

This approach to leadership is from the believe that "today

Terry Sloan

is so interconnected and interdependent that leaders need to differentiate situations that are Complex from those that are complicated – think Everglades (Complex) versus Rolex watch (complicated) or customer relations (Complex) versus financial spreadsheet (complicated

CONCEPTS OF LEADERSHIP

Leaders are made not born. If you have the desire and willpower, you can become an effective leader.

Good leaders develop through a never ending process of self-study, education, training, and experience. To say in in another way "Leadership can be taught" all you need to do is be a willing and open student.

This guide will help you through that process.

To inspire your workers into higher levels of teamwork, there are certain things you must be, know, and, do. These do not come naturally, but are acquired through continual work and study.

Good leaders are continually working and studying to improve their leadership skills; they are NOT resting on their laurels.

Leadership is a process by which a person influences others to accomplish an objective and directs the organization in a way that makes it more cohesive and coherent. Leaders carry out this process by applying their leadership attributes, such as beliefs, values, ethics, character, knowledge, and skills.

Although your position as a manager, supervisor, lead, etc. gives you the authority to accomplish certain tasks and objectives in the organization, this power does not make you a leader, it simply makes you the boss.

Leadership differs in that it makes the followers want to achieve high goals, rather than simply bossing people around.

Bass' (1989 & 1990) theory of leadership states that there are three basic ways to explain how people become leaders. The first two explain the leadership development for a small number of people. These theories are: Some personality traits may lead people naturally into leadership roles. This is the Trait Theory.

A crisis or important event may cause a person to rise to the occasion, which brings out extraordinary leadership qualities in an ordinary person. This is the Great Events Theory.

People can choose to become leaders. People can learn leadership skills. This is the Transformational Leadership Theory. It is the most widely accepted theory today and the premise on which this guide is based.

When a person is deciding if They respects you as a leader, They do not think about your attributes, rather, They observe what you do so that They can know who you really are. They use this observation to tell if you are an honorable and trusted leader or a self-serving person who misuses authority to look good and get promoted. Self-serving leaders are not as effective because their employees only obey them, not follow them. There is often no respect or buy in to the Leaders vision. There is only fear of losing their position. Bad Leaders succeed in many areas only because they present a good image to their seniors at the expense of their workers.

The basis of good leadership is honorable character and selfless service to your organization. In your employees' eyes, your leadership is everything you do that effects the organization's objectives and their well-being. Respected leaders concentrate on what they are [be] (such as beliefs and character), what they know (such as job, tasks, and human nature), and what they do (such as implementing, motivating, and providing direction).

What makes a person want to follow a leader? People want to

be guided by those they respect and who have a clear sense of direction. To gain respect, they must be ethical. A sense of direction is achieved by conveying a strong vision of the future.

FACTORS OF LEADERSHIP

There are four major factors in leadership:

Follower:

Different people require different styles of leadership. For example, a new hire requires more supervision than an experienced employee. A person who lacks motivation requires a different approach than one with a high degree of motivation. You must know your people! The fundamental starting point is having a good understanding of human nature, such as needs, emotions, and motivation. You must come to know your employees' be, know, and do attributes.

Leader:

You must have an honest understanding of who you are, what you know, and what you can do. Also, note that it is the followers, not the leader who determines if a leader is successful. If they do not trust or lack confidence in their leader, then they will be uninspired. To be successful you have to convince your followers, not yourself or your superiors, that you are worthy of being followed.

Communication:

You lead through two-way communication. Much of it is nonverbal. For instance, when you "set the example," that communicates to your people that you would not ask them to perform anything that you would not be willing to do. What and how you communicate either builds or harms the relationship between you and your employees.

Situation:

All are different. What you do in one situation will not always work in another. You must use your judgment to decide the best course of action and the leadership style needed for each situation. For example, you may need to confront an employee for inappropriate behavior, but if the confrontation is too late or too early, too harsh or too weak, then the results may prove ineffective.

Various forces will affect these factors. Examples of forces are your relationship with your seniors, the skill of your people, the informal leaders within your organization, and how your company is organized.

Attributes:

If you are a leader who can be trusted, then those around you will grow to respect you. To be such a leader, there is a Leadership Framework to guide you: BE KNOW DO

- BE a professional. Examples: Be loyal to the organization, perform selfless service, take personal responsibility.
- BE a professional who possess good character traits. Examples: Honesty, competence, candor, commitment, integrity, courage, straightforwardness, imagination.
- KNOW the four factors of leadership - follower, leader,

- communication, situation.
- KNOW yourself. Examples: strengths and weakness of your character, knowledge, and skills.
- KNOW human nature. Examples: Human needs, emotions, and how people respond to stress.
- KNOW your job. Examples: be proficient and be able to train others in their tasks.
- KNOW your organization. Examples: where to go for help, its climate and culture, who the unofficial leaders are.
- DO provide direction. Examples: goal setting, problem solving, decision making, planning.

DO implement. Examples: communicating, coordinating, supervising, evaluating.

- DO motivate. Examples: develop morale and esprit de corps in the organization, train, coach, counsel.

-

Environment:

Every organization has a particular work environment, which dictates to a considerable degree how its

leaders respond to problems and opportunities. This is brought about by its heritage of past leaders and its present leaders. Goals, Values, and Concepts

Leaders exert influence on the environment via three types of actions:

- The goals and performance standards they establish.
- The values they establish for the organization.
- The business and people concepts they establish.

Successful organizations have leaders who set high standards and goals across the entire spectrum, such as strategies, market leadership, plans, meetings and presentations, productivity, quality, and reliability.

Values reflect the concern the organization has for its employees, customers, investors, vendors, and surrounding community. These values define the manner in how business will be conducted.

Concepts define what products or services the organization will offer and the methods and processes for conducting business.

These goals, values, and concepts make up the organization's "personality" or how the organization is

observed by both outsiders and insiders. This personality defines the roles, relationships, rewards, and rites that take place.

Roles and Relationships:

Roles are the positions that are defined by a set of expectations about behavior of any job incumbent.

Each role has a set of tasks and responsibilities that may or may not be spelled out. Roles have a powerful effect on behavior for several reasons, to include money being paid for the performance of the role, there is prestige attached to a role, and a sense of accomplishment or challenge.

Relationships are determined by a role's tasks. While some tasks are performed alone, most are carried out in relationship with others. The tasks will determine who the role-holder is required to interact with, how often, and towards what end. Also, normally the greater the interaction, the greater the liking. This in turn leads to more frequent interaction. In human behavior, it's hard to like someone whom we have no contact with, and we tend to seek out those we like. People tend to do what they are rewarded for, and friendship is a powerful reward. Many tasks and behaviors that are associated with a role are brought about by these relationships. That is, new task and behaviors are expected of the present role-holder because a strong relationship was developed in the past, either by that role-holder or a prior role-holder.

Culture and Climate:

There are two distinct forces that dictate how to act within an organization: culture and climate.

Each organization has its own distinctive culture. It is a combination of the founders, past leadership, current leadership, crises, events, history, and size. This results in rites: the routines, rituals, and the "way

we do things." These rites impact individual behavior on what it takes to be in good standing (the norm) and directs the appropriate behavior for each circumstance.

The climate is the feel of the organization, the individual and shared perceptions and attitudes of the organization's members. While the culture is the deeply rooted nature of the organization that is a result of long-held formal and informal systems, rules, traditions, and customs; climate is a short-term phenomenon created by the current leadership. Climate represents the beliefs about the "feel of the organization" by its members. This individual perception of the "feel of the organization" comes from

what the people believe about the activities that occur in the organization. These activities influence both individual and team motivation and satisfaction, such as:

How well does the leader clarify the priorities and goals of the organization? What is expected of us?

What is the system of recognition, rewards, and punishments in the organization?

- How competent are the leaders?
- Are leaders free to make decisions?
- What will happen if I make a mistake?

Organizational climate is directly related to the leadership and management style of the leader, based on the values, attributes, skills, and actions, as well as the priorities of the leader. Compare this to "ethical climate" the "feel of the organization" about the activities that have ethical content or those aspects of the work environment that constitute ethical behavior. The ethical climate is the feel about whether we do things right; or the feel of whether we behave the way we ought to behave. The behavior (character) of the leader is the most important factor that impacts the climate.

On the other hand, culture is a long-term, complex phenomenon. Culture represents the shared expectations and self-image of the organization. The mature values that create "tradition" or the "way we do things here." Things are done differently in every organization. The collective vision and common folklore that define the institution are a reflection of culture. Individual leaders, cannot easily create or change culture because culture is a part of the organization. Culture influences the characteristics of the climate by its effect on the actions and thought processes of the leader. But, everything you do as a leader will affect the climate of the organization.

Leadership Models:

Leadership models help us to understand what makes leaders act the way they do. The ideal is not to lock yourself in to a type of behavior discussed in the model, but to realize that every situation calls for a different approach or behavior to be taken. Two models will be discussed, the Four Framework Approach and the Managerial Grid.

Four Framework Approach

In the Four Framework Approach, Bolman and Deal (1991) suggest that leaders display leadership behaviors in one of four types of frameworks: Structural, Human Resource, Political, or Symbolic. The style can either be effective or ineffective, depending upon the chosen behavior in certain situations.

Structural Framework

In an effective leadership situation, the leader is a social architect whose leadership style is analysis and design. While in an ineffective leadership situation, the leader is a petty tyrant whose leadership style is details. Structural Leaders focus on structure, strategy, environment, implementation, experimentation, and adaptation.

Human Resource Framework

In an effective leadership situation, the leader is a catalyst and servant whose leadership style is support, advocation, and empowerment. While in an ineffective leadership situation, the leader is a pushover, whose leadership style is abdication and fraud. Human Resource Leaders believe in people and communicate that belief; they are visible and accessible; they empower, increase participation, support, share information, and move decision making down into the organization.

Political Framework

In an effective leadership situation, the leader is an advocate, whose leadership style is coalition and building. While in an ineffective leadership situation, the leader is a hustler, whose leadership style is manipulation. Political leaders clarify what they want and what they can get; they assess the distribution of power and interests; they build linkages to other stakeholders, use persuasion first, then use negotiation and coercion only if necessary.

Symbolic Framework

In an effective leadership situation, the leader is a prophet, whose leadership style is inspiration. While in an ineffective leadership situation, the leader is a fanatic or fool, whose leadership style is smoke and mirrors. Symbolic leaders view organizations as a stage or theater to play certain roles and give impressions; these leaders use symbols to capture attention; they try to frame experience by providing plausible interpretations of experiences; they discover and communicate a vision.

This model suggests that leaders can be put into one of these four categories and there are times when one approach is appropriate and times when it would not be. Any one of these approaches alone would be inadequate, thus we should strive to be conscious of all four approaches, and not just rely on one or two. For example, during a major organization change, a structural leadership style may be more effective than a visionary leadership style; while during a period when strong growth is needed, the visionary approach may be better. We also need to understand ourselves as each of us tends to have a preferred approach. We need to be conscious of this at all times and be aware of the limitations of our favoring just one approach.

Authoritarian Leader (high task, low relationship)

People who get this rating are very much task oriented and are hard on their workers (autocratic). There is little or no allowance for cooperation or collaboration. Heavily task oriented people display these characteristics: they are very strong on schedules; they expect people to do what they are told without question or debate; when something goes wrong they tend to focus on who is to blame rather than concentrate on exactly what is wrong and how to prevent it; they are intolerant of what they see as dissent (it may just be someone's creativity), so it is difficult for their subordinates to contribute or develop.

Team Leader (high task, high relationship)

This type of person leads by positive example and endeavors to foster a team environment in which all team members can reach their highest potential, both as team members and as people. They encourage the team to reach team goals as effectively as possible, while also working tirelessly to strengthen the bonds among the various members. They normally form and lead some of the most productive teams.

Country Club Leader (low task, high relationship)

This person uses predominantly reward power to maintain discipline and to encourage the team to accomplish its goals. Conversely, they are almost incapable of employing the more punitive coercive and legitimate powers. This inability results from fear that using such powers could jeopardize relationships with the other team members.

Impoverished Leader (low task, low relationship)

A leader who uses a "delegate and disappear" management style. Since they are not committed to either task accomplishment or maintenance; they essentially allow their team to do whatever it wishes and prefer to detach themselves from the team process by allowing the team to suffer from a series of power struggles.

The most desirable place for a leader to be along the two axes at most times would be a 9 on task and a 9 on people -- the Team Leader. However, do not entirely dismiss the other three. Certain situations might call for one of the other three to be used at times. For example, by playing the Impoverished Leader, you allow your team to gain self-reliance. Be an Authoritarian Leader to instill a sense of discipline in an unmotivated worker. By carefully studying the situation and the forces affecting it, you will know at what points along the axes you need to be in order to achieve the desired result.

The Process of Great Leadership

The road to great leadership (Kouzes & Posner, 1987) that is common to successful leaders:

Challenge the process - First, find a process that you believe needs to be improved the most.

Inspire a shared vision - Next, share your vision in words that can be understood by your followers.

Enable others to act - Give them the tools and methods to solve the problem.

Model the way - When the process gets tough, get your hands dirty. A boss tells others what to do, a leader shows that it can be done. Encourage the heart - Share the glory with your followers' hearts, while

keeping the pains within your own.

WAYS OF DEFINING LEADERSHIP

Leadership means being the dominant individual in a group.

In primitive tribes and higher animal species the dominant individual was the leader. Being the leader simply meant having the power to attain and hold the top position for a reasonable length of time, you could be the leader without getting anything done through others. A leader was the person in charge even if the group was in a stable state where people went about their business as normal. As long as group members obeyed the leader's rules, the leader did not even need to be actively involved in the lives of group members, let alone get anything done through them. You could also be the leader in such a group without promoting a better way as suggested by definition 3. If you didn't need to be voted into power, why have a platform for change? You simply seized power; no sales pitch was needed on how you could make life better for the group. Yes, such leaders may have led groups successfully in battle and built great monuments with them, but, strictly speaking, you could be the leader without achieving anything through a group effort. The meaning of leadership, according to this definition, is simply to be at the top of the pile.

Leadership means getting things done through people.

Great leaders throughout history have led their groups to momentous achievements, but the idea that leadership should be defined as getting things done through people has been developed most fully by modern business, which is all about achieving results. As business has become more complex, the leadership challenge has grown form one of the simple issuing of orders to a few "hands" to the subtle coordination of highly skilled, diverse knowledge workers to build sophisticated machines and put men on the moon. There is a problem with this definition of leadership, however. It used to belong to management. Why the switch from management to leadership? And is this a good move? Up to the late 1970's writers used the terms leadership and management interchangeably but with more emphasis on management. For example, the management theorists, Blake and Mouton, developed their famous managerial grid in the 1960's. At the time, it was portrayed as a way of identifying your management style. Today, in line with the shift to leadership, the name is the same (managerial grid) but it is now positioned as a leadership style instrument.

Similarly, we used to talk about management style more than leadership style. Managers could be either "theory X" and task oriented or "theory Y" and concerned for people. But a profound shift in thinking took place in a revolutionary period lasting from the late 1970's through the mid 1980's. The cause of this upheaval was the commercial success of Japanese industry in North America. This led pundits to claim that the U.S.

had lost its competitive edge because U.S. management was too bureaucratic, controlling, uninspiring and inept at fostering innovation. Rather than upgrade management, there was an emotional over reaction such that management was rejected and replaced by leadership. Since then, leaders were portrayed as theory Y, inspiring and concerned about people while management got saddled with all the bad guy attributes of being controlling, theory X, uninspiring and narrowly task focused. Similarly, the distinction between being transformational and transactional was originally launched to differentiate two leadership styles, but it wasn't long before it became used to separate leadership from management, the former being transformational and the latter transactional.

In our haste to trash management, we grabbed whatever tools were handy but with heavy costs. First, we painted leadership into a corner by suggesting that you needed to be an inspiring cheerleader to be a leader, leaving no room for quiet or simply factual leadership. Second, we created a bloated concept of leadership by banishing management. Third, by attaching leadership to getting things done through a team, we associated leadership irrevocably with being in charge of people, thereby ruling out positionless leadership. Yes, there is informal leadership but this concept is essentially the same as formal leadership except for their power bases. Like its formal counterpart, informal leadership still means taking charge and managing a group to achieve a target. In either case, you need to have the personal presence, organizational skills and motivation to take charge to be a leader.

Leadership means challenging the status quo, promoting a better way.

We have always felt, intuitively, that leaders have the courage to stand up and be counted. They go against the grain, often at great risk, to call for change. We only need to look at Martin Luther

King, Jr. His leadership rested not so much on his oratorical skills - they were just icing on the cake. He was a leader primarily because he marched and spoke against injustice. He challenged the status quo and promoted a better world.

However, and this is the whole point here, if you think through what it means to challenge the status quo or advocate change, there is no necessary implication that you have to be in charge of the people you are trying to influence. The bottom line is that this third definition, when worked through fully, gives us a way to break the stranglehold of the previous two definitions. The benefit of this move is that we gain a clearer understanding of how all employees can show leadership even if they totally lack the skills or inclination to take charge of groups in a managerial sense, even informally. Think again of Martin Luther King, Jr. He sought to move the U.S. Government and the population at large to think differently about such issues as segregation on buses. His leadership efforts were successful when the U.S. Supreme Court ruled such discrimination unconstitutional. Now, it is obvious that he was not in a managerial role within the Supreme Court. He showed leadership to this group as an outsider. You could say the same of Jack Welch who had a leadership impact on countless businesses around the globe through his novel practices, such as being first or second in a market.

Key Features of Leadership

It does not involve managing people to get things done.

It comes to an end once those led get on board. It sells the tickets for the journey; management drives the bus to the destination.

It is a discrete episode, a one-off act of influence, not an ongoing position of dominance.

It is based on the promotion of a better way.

It can be shown bottom-up as well as top-down.

It can be shown by outsiders and between competing individuals or groups.

The Essence of Leadership

Organizations today need all employees to think creatively and to promote new products. Promoting a better idea can be called thought leadership. In a knowledge driven environment, the newest, best idea influences others to get on board. When a product developer convinces top management to adopt a new product, that person has shown thought leadership bottom-up. But it can be shown across groups as well.

While the possession of great emotional intelligence and the oratory of a Martin Luther King, Jr. can help thought leaders make their case, it is vital to see that these skills are nice to have add-ons, not an essential part of the meaning of leadership. Technical geeks with zero emotional intelligence and an obnoxious influencing style can show thought leadership if they can demonstrate the value of their ideas. This is very empowering because it moves us away from the demand to develop sophisticated leadership skills as a precondition of showing leadership.

Strictly speaking there are no leadership skills, only influencing skills and great content. Imagine asking Tiger Woods. after the end of the third round when he is in the lead, how he developed such great leadership skills. The truth is that he shows leadership through being great at the content of his profession, not by having a separate set of talents called leadership skills. On the other hand, there are very definite management skills. Getting work done through people calls for quite sophisticated interpersonal and organizational skills.

A STAND

If you want to serve as a leader, then actually act like one, and be a leader. That means a leader must step forward while others stand on the sideline. Judge someone as a leader not by what they do regarding popular programs and ideas. Rather they must be judged by whether or not they stand up for what they believe, and take what are often difficult or challenging positions. Certainly it is challenging and even stressful at times to stand alone on principle, if you really believe in something. Leadership is about inner strength and fortitude, and doing and saying what needs to be do e, even if it may at times be unpopular or out of fashion.

1. I recall serving for nearly a decade, many years ago, as the Treasurer of a non profit. it seemed obvious to me that this particular organization, if it did not take steps to address putting

their financial house in order, would soon be facing the prospect of insolvency. Although I was often overwhelmingly opposed, I continued to chastise, coerce, and demand that the Board acted responsibly. Years later, almost every one of my proposals was enacted, and although waiting as long as they did had a negative overall compacted fiscal and financial impact, the fact that they eventually did what was needed guaranteed the road to solvency and relevance. The interesting aspect, however, is that the very same people who openly bad mouthed me, and derided my point of view, eventually championed the battle, and were more than glad to take full credit for the accomplishment. However, the important thing is not who got the credit, but that what needed to get done, did.

2. Leadership must never be about one's ego or popularity. Rather, it is about webbing effectively, and bringing an organization to achieve and perform to its potential, and to accomplish worthwhile missions. Great leaders always begin with a vital vision, and that vision always acts to motivate them to commit to a greater extent, try harder, care more, and make more efforts to include others in the quest. The true mark of a great leader is not only getting followers to care, but developing the ones with the most potential, to become future true leaders.

LEADERS ALWAYS CELEBRATE SMALL WINS

Every success is a success, and great leaders recognize the small wins just as often as they recognize the big ones. Celebrating everything worth celebrating makes work better for everyone in a few noteworthy ways.

Creating a Sense of Unity

There are some natural disconnects, particularly in communication, between leaders and the people they lead. When you're willing to celebrate the small victories, you're reminding your team members that you stand in solidarity with them. They feel relieved and happy when they've successfully met any challenge, no matter the size. You should too. It shows that they're growing in their skills and competency, and celebrating that shows that you're involved enough to know the kind of progress that they're making on the ground.

Keeping Employees Happy

Everyone is susceptible to burnout. If it's difficult to see the payoff from all of the hard work you've been doing, that makes it even harder to continue doing that work.

Small celebrations show your team members that their efforts are worthwhile. They're being recognized, rather than being ushered from one task directly into another. That small break in the day provides them with the opportunity for introspection. They can reflect on the skills they used to accomplish what they accomplished and feel good about their work.

Inspiring Greater Productivity

The necessity of keeping employees at a high level of productivity is one of the most important things they teach you in management school. What they don't always teach you is the variety of methods you can use to achieve that goal. The idea of reward encourages people to be productive. That's why it feels better to walk to the ice cream shop than it does to walk home from it.

If your employees know they'll have an opportunity to enjoy something fun after they've put in the efforts, they're more likely to work more efficiently in order to meet the goal in a timely manner.

Making The Work Environment Positive

Tensions and rivalries arise in the workplace from time to time – especially if your workplace is well staffed. Having a diverse group of people with opposing viewpoints and different experiences can help your team function better, because everyone has something unique that they bring to the table. The interactions won't always be pretty, and that's why small celebrations are important. They keep things lighthearted, particularly after some of the spirited debates your team members may have encountered while completing a project.

Boosting Motivation

Company culture is so important. If your culture involves celebration and recognition, your employees will have a constant reminder of what they're working towards, and that the people around them share the same professional values. A thriving company culture builds teams that want to stick together for the long haul, even when things get particularly stressful or something doesn't work out the way it was planned.

You want your team members to love their jobs that's what ultimately gives them the strength to keep going, even in the darkest of times. Celebrating will motivate them by encouraging them to hold on to that hope and reminding them of the reasons why they're doing what they're doing.

Great leaders will never miss an opportunity to celebrate, even over things that might seem trivial on a surface level. As long as your celebration is proportional to the achievement, there's no way to do it wrong, and no excuse to skip the joy.

REASONS WHY LEADERS SHOULD CELEBRATE WINS

Celebrating the wins can be beneficial in many ways when it comes to business. Read on to find out the top 10 reasons why leaders should relish in the successes.

1. Acknowledges progress

Celebrating a win is a great way to acknowledge progress towards achieving a goal. Whether they've reached the halfway point or gotten to the finish line, it shows the team that great progress has been made. That feeling of accomplishment will drive everyone to work even harder towards the next goal.

2. Builds momentum

Everyone thrives off the exhilaration that comes from a win and celebrating it leaves people wanting more. Leaders who celebrate wins will notice a definite charge in the energy of their people because after every great win, they'll be doing everything they can to experience that feeling again.

3. Accentuates the positive

Although there will be times when you have to point out what went wrong, shining the spotlight on what went right always yields great results. Celebrating the wins actually increases the likelihood there will be more wins simply because positivity feels good.

4. Inspires more good work

When somebody tells you, "Hey, that color looks great on you," you run out and buy 5 more shirts in that exact color. When you celebrate the wins, it sends a message to your team that they're doing something right. This will motivate them to do great work over and over again.

5. Gives hope

Life and work are challenging. Yet within all of us there's that one fundamental element that keeps us going hope. When you celebrate the wins, you're instilling a sense of hope within your team because each win motivates the next. Even those team members who are struggling with challenges will be inspired when you take the time to acknowledge the smallest win.

6. A break from the daily grind

However you celebrate, whether with a happy hour at the local pub or lunch for the crew in the break room, you're transporting your team to a different state of mind. That change, even if just for an hour from work to party mode, breathes new life and energy into their souls. This gives your team the time to refresh and prepare to work towards another win.

7. Creates a sense of pride

We've all belted our hearts out to Queen's We Are the Champions. It's not just because it's a catchy tune, but also because it just feels so good to be on the winning team. When you celebrate wins, it fosters a sense of pride within your team that will motivate them to work towards future greatness.

8. Attracts others to your team

Everyone wants to be on the winning team, especially when they see how much fun you have while celebrating. Your team will be even more driven to work towards their next win once they know others are watching.

9. Brings the team together

Nothing unifies a group of people more than a celebration of achieving a common goal. With a unified team, you can enhance the effectiveness of a group that knows the strengths and weaknesses of each member.

10. Creates a winning culture

Fewer things are more uplifting than knowing you're a part of something successful. By incorporating celebrations into your company culture, you're ingraining the idea that success leads to more success.

As the leader of your team, make it a point to celebrate the wins whenever possible. You'll not only bring happiness to your employees, but you'll also help improve the performance, productivity and opportunity for more success. Even celebrating the smallest wins can greatly increase morale within your team.

GREAT LEADERS TAKE THE BLAME AND PASS ON THE CREDIT

Even when they fail, great leaders believe in their abilities. Acknowledging and learning from mistakes allows you to lead by example, and encourages your team to see mistakes not as the end of the line, but as the beginning of growth.

I have seen time and again how the committed take responsibility for their actions. In our high-litigation culture, there's always someone else to blame. It can be easy to point the finger at suppliers, underlings, partners, and managers that just can't seem to get things right. I have yet to meet this mass of completely incompetent workers, which leads me to think we might be trying to steer some of the fault away from where it belongs--onto ourselves.

True leaders pull the thumb, before they point the finger

They take responsibility... for Everything. They turn each misstep into an opportunity to learn from the mistake instead of pointing figures: they pull the thumb and ask themselves "what could I have done differently?" They find a lesson while others only see a problem. They privately address their subordinates' mistakes with them, but take the blame publicly without dissent. If someone slipped up, they pick them up, they don't point the finger and pass the blame.

Leaders pass the credit and take the blame

An effective leader is someone who inspires those beneath them. If you pass blame and take credit, if your team clocks in at nine and checks out at five, if they make no mistakes and only send you finely-crafted emails and reports, congratulations, you're a manager. Not a leader. Leaders recognize that an inspired team not only produces great work, but regularly strive beyond that extra mile to ensure success. Passing credit onto those under you is the best, and the easiest, way to do this. Why? A leader is nothing without their team.

In classical warfare, if an army loses, is it because a single person failed in his duties, or turned coat too early? No. More likely it was because they were in the wrong position, advanced too early, or what have you.

If an army wins, is it because one unit, or one captain, made a daring charge, or was in the right place at the right time? No. It is because every single person performed admirably in each of their roles.

See the difference? Failures are often the result of bad leadership, and passing the blame onto those beneath them is not only misplaced, but discouraging. Successes, on the other hand, are wholly based on the performance of every individual effort. And assuming the credit for oneself is not only selfish, but alienating. Managers fight battles, leaders win wars.

The first step to finding a solution to a problem is admitting you have a problem. From my experience, the reluctance of good leaders to accept the blame for mistakes has its roots in two misconceptions of what mistakes really are.

Mistakes are an opportunity

A common error is assuming that once a mistake has been committed, or revealed, that it is the end of the line. Work often screeches to a halt while the extent of the mistake is exposed, and the culprit brought to justice. All hands are called to the pumps in order to craft a solution in secret, away from judging eyes.

This unfortunate habit leaders have picked up instills a natural fear of mistakes in everyone. Mistakes should not be feared, but expected, and often encouraged. They should be used as an opportunity to teach team members, new employees, interns, and managers.

Leaders who expect one-hundred per-cent perfection from their team will not only work in a very silent office, but receive late emails, and stifle creativity. Why? Because people are naturally afraid of making mistakes, being called out, and being embarrassed in public. A leader who assumes the blame, and passes the credit, sends a message that mistakes are OK, and that when they happen it will be an opportunity to learn and grow. By inspiring those beneath you, your employees will emulate your best traits, which will include assuming the blame for themselves.

Mistakes are NOT failures

A fatal flaw in modern leadership is equating mistakes with failure. Without waxing trite, I will refrain from numerous anecdotes relating the importance of "getting back on the horse" or "we only truly fail when we give up"; all are applicable. The moral hazard in not differentiating the two is employees who almost expect the assignment to be taken from them the moment a mistake is committed and reassigned to someone else. Because a failure means the end of their contribution. It's done.

However, ensuring that you understand the difference, and that your employees do, too, results in everyone recognizing that mistakes are to be remedied by those who erred, with the expectation that the stewardship was given to them to complete a task, and a mistake does not invalidate that trust. Associating failure with mistakes demonstrates a lack of trust in those to whom you delegate. But by allowing employees to internalize the responsibility given to them, it becomes easier to give credit where it is due.

Leaders pull the thumb instead of point fingers. They inspire and encourage. They are perceptive and honest. If a leader is truly transparent for a moment, they will recognize they truly had no claim on any of the credit at all in the first place. Instead, a true leader can see the minute contributions that everyone has made to their success. So, in truth, being a good leader is really just learning to be a decent human being. And that is easy enough.

A GOOD LEADER

A strong leadership and good managerial skills can go a long way in ascertaining the company's profits. As far as leadership is concerned, there are two schools of thoughts, which try to explain how leaders "happen." The first thought states that strong leaders are not made, but rather they are born. It may have to do something with the genes or the family atmosphere, which induces leadership qualities in a person. The other thought is more practical, and states that leaders can be made after carefully grooming individuals and teaching them correct managerial skills and leadership qualities. While it may not be possible to make a leader out of every individual, it is certainly possible to train a few individuals to become leaders if they have the potential to learn the qualities. The bottom line is whether you are a born leader, or a groomed one, you need to exhibit strong leadership qualities and efficient managerial abilities to lead a team in a successful manner. A couple of points may help you to understand how leaders are made.

- **Be humane**

There is a subtle way in which authority should be delegated to the subordinates. Contrary to the misconception, good leadership is not considering your juniors as individuals lacking in qualities, or thinking about them as deprived individuals. Authority should be delegated in a firm manner, but at all times the person should consider the team members as important entities for the functioning of the business, and not indispensable commodities. Respecting another person can go a long way in earning that person's respect, and people tend to obey and follow orders when they feel respected.

- **Be a role model**

It is always easy to speak than to act. While most leaders and managers tend to issue orders and wait patiently for them to be completed, employees usually respect leaders when they lay down an example by doing the work themselves. Of course, you don't need to work on behalf of your employees, but setting up an example once in a while can help to convey the message that you are not the sitting type and won't tolerate inefficiency. Setting up examples can encourage others to follow suit.

- **Be genuine**

While individuals can use their charisma to attract people and fool them into thinking you are an excellent leader, the truth will most likely emerge sooner or later. It is better to be genuine and not put on an act. People will respect you more, and believe you

Terry Sloan

if you appear to be genuine, and a type of person who believes no one is perfect, but by being careful and methodical one can be close to being perfect.

5 COMMON TRAITS OF GREAT LEADERSHIP

Vision – Therefore, great leaders must have vision, this is absolutely critical. Without vision and knowing the path they are taking, how is one able to effectively lead? Leaders must be able to motivate and inspire people to action, and they can do so through communicating their vision in a compelling, passionate and clear manner. A leader who can do this is able to motivate people into acting with passion and purpose, ensuring that everyone is working toward a common goal, preventing the company and team members from moving in different directions. The result? Everyone contributes to the forward momentum of the organization.

Communication – it's an absolute fundamental leadership skill. This is how ideas, results and information are shared, initiatives implemented and so much more. Communication is about more than just relaying information, it's also, and perhaps more importantly about listening. Great leaders listen and recognize that this is a fundamental piece of their communication skills.

Delegation – Simply put, great leaders are great at delegating. Delegation is about more than just getting things off of your plate. Doing big things means getting work done through yourself and others you can't do it all by yourself, and you're not necessarily the best suited to lead every task. Delegation is about recognizing who has the best skills to manage, lead and organize specific projects, and trusting them to do so.

Decision Making – This is probably the most basic duty that any leader must tend to. To be highly effective, you can't be afraid to make tough decisions on the fly. Great leaders also stick to their decisions once they're made, unless something comes up and dictates otherwise.

Integrity – Employees want to trust the individuals that set the tone, pace and direction of their place of employment, after all, they spend a great deal of their time there, doing their part to make the company succeed. To gain that trust, leaders must have integrity, be fair and honest, treating individuals as they would like to be treated

IMPORTANCE OF LEADERSHIP FOR ORGANIZATION

The classic model of the good organizational leader is the top executive in the organizational management who directs and who is in control of all aspects of the operations of the organization. This top executive leader operates through a hierarchy of management and the organization had a fairly well defined structure. This type of leadership has some good points and it survived throughout most of the 20th century.

The organization of today does not have the luxury of stability since it faces an ever increasing change in markets, customers and technology. It needs to accept, adopt and implement changes in the business model according to changing trends, technologies, customer preferences and future concerns. Further, the core business of the organization is constantly under threat today from the newcomers to the marketplace who are having a different business paradigm. Hence the organization cannot afford to depend upon the leadership of individual or/and a small team of senior executives to meet this challenge. The organization needs to harness the ideas, skills, energy, and enthusiasm of the entire team for success. For meeting of new challenges, this new concept and practice of leadership has evolved, where line managers have taken over the leadership role along with the top executive and his small team of senior executives.

Leadership is an important factor for making an organization successful. It is the art or process of influencing people to perform assigned tasks willingly, efficiently and competently. Without leadership a line manager simply cannot be effective. Leadership of the line managers transforms potential into reality. When good leadership is in place in the organization, it can be felt throughout the entire organization. With good leadership, organizational culture is not forced but developed. Communication is effective and open. Everyone understands the vision and goals of the organization, and everyone has input into how they can be improved. People feel that they are an important part of the organization and they give their best for the success of the organization.

The leadership in the organization is to meet the three challenges. The first challenge is to provide a shared vision of where the organisation is heading and what its purpose is (the mission). The second challenge is to set objectives, that is, to convert the strategic vision and directional course into specific performance outcomes for each key area which leaders deem important for success. The third challenge in providing strategic direction is to generate and develop a strategy that will determine how to achieve the objectives. Strategic direction is imperative in identifying a systematic intervention that will provide the most leverage to the organisation, as an organisation cannot focus on everything all of the time.

Line manager leaders are a key human resource in the organization. These leaders develop better people under them and the two together develop better products which can compete effectively with the products offered by the competitors. We generally think of organizations competing by means of their products, but today organizations probably compete more by means of the quality of their line manager leaders than their products.

High performance of people in the organization is the focal point for achieving success. This high performance can be secured only if there is effective leadership qualities available with the lines managers.

As group efforts and teamwork are essential for realizing the organizational goals, leadership becomes vital for the execution of work. Through leadership, line managers can influence people under them to adopt a cooperative and wholesome attitude for successful work accomplishment. Their leadership motivates the people to a higher level of performance through their strong human relations.

Leadership is an important function of management which helps to maximize efficiency and to achieve organizational goals. In fact leadership is an essential part and a crucial component of effective management. A remarkable leadership behaviour stresses upon building an environment in which each and every employee develops and excels. It has the potential to influence and drive the group efforts towards the accomplishment of goals. Line managers must have traits of a leader. They must possess leadership qualities. With leadership qualities line managers can develop and begin strategies that build and sustain competitive advantage.

The following are some of the ways which demonstrate the importance of leadership for the achievement of the organizational excellence.

One of the first steps that the leaders in the organization need to undertake is to establish why the organization exists and what it wants to achieve. Leaders are to clarify and communicate the vision and mission of the organization to the people. This vision and mission effectively provides employees with an understanding of the organizational direction and allows them to clearly understand their roles and responsibilities.

Leaders communicate the policies and plans to the people of the organization. They are to imbibe the values and the culture of the organization since these play an important role in ensuring the achievement of the organizational goals.

Leaders provide a structured approach. The structured approach is able to generate a plan of action that most effectively meets the organizational goals. An inclusive planning process also provides the opportunity for people to identify, contribute to, understand and achieve well defined objectives.

The commitment and enthusiasm of leaders shape the common goals of the organization and provides inspiration and motivation for people to perform at a high level.

Leaders provide encouragement to people for openly contributing and discussing new ideas in a positive environment and make use of their diverse experience and ideas to improve the organization.

Leaders have an open and engaging relationship with the people. This relationship demonstrates that the people are valued as an integral part of the organization, creates a sense of ownership among people, and develops a closer alignment between individual and organizational objectives.

Good leadership can help the organization remain focused during a time of crisis, reminding the people of their achievements and encourage them to set short term, achievable goals.

There are differences between leadership and management functions. Leadership provides direction, encouragement and inspiration to motivate a team to achieve organizational success. Management is primarily an organizational role, coordinating the efforts of the people and the allocation of resources to maximize efficiency in achieving identified goals.

Leadership and management are closely linked functions. Both the functions are complimentary to each other. Without efficient management, the direction set by a leader risks being unsustainable. Similarly, management exercised without effective leadership perpetuates current activities and directions, without adaptation to meet strategic goals and without optimizing the performance of the organization.

Leadership and management operate hand in hand. To be a good manager, line managers require leadership skills, and an effective leader depends on the management skills for achieving the goals and objectives.

Effective leadership of the line managers requires leadership qualities in them. These qualities are to be visible by their actions in the context and circumstances of different situations. Line managers with effective leadership qualities exhibit a combination of some of the following qualities.

Leadership qualities of line managers

These qualities are described below.

Future vision- Successful leadership involves creating a well founded vision of what can be achieved in the future and the best way to approach it.

Integrity – Effective leaders often place great importance on ethical values. They always do the right things even if these things are difficult. In general, leaders with integrity are honest, truthful, fair, reliable and do not let their emotions affect their ability to do their job.

Self confidence – Good and strong leaders have a firm belief in their abilities. They generally remain confident at all the times and demonstrate the ability to handle challenges and pressures.

Commitment – Successful leadership is impossible without firm commitment. Good leaders remain focused and dedicated towards their objectives and goals.

Creativity – Effective line managers with the leadership qualities are creative in their approach. They develop new ideas to resolve current issues and implement them effectively to prevent future recurrences.

Communication skill – Communication skill is vital for effective leadership. Lines managers with leadership qualities are usually very clear, effective and influential in communication and knows its importance for achieving success. They continuously improve their communication skills and learn new ways to remain effective in a constantly changing organizational environment.

Enthusiasm – Effective leadership normally requires a proactive approach towards people, problems and possibilities. It is able to stimulate and evoke excitement amongst people so that the organizational goals can be achieved in an energetic manner.

Self awareness and adaptability – Line managers who are skilful leaders exhibit an understanding of their own values, skills, strengths and weaknesses. They are often flexible and willing to continually improve their knowledge and skills to meet new challenges.

Decision making capabilities – This is the capability to exploit opportunities and to make sound decisions which benefits the organization. Line managers with leadership qualities have the capabilities for making sound decisions.

Openness – Line managers with effective leadership qualities listen openly to the ideas, suggestions and opinions of their people. They are willing to adopt new ways of doing things if they believe it will be beneficial for the organisation. They focus on creating a positive environment of mutual respect and trust that enables the organization to be well prepared for new challenges.

Ability to understand people – Good leadership amongst line managers requires a clear understanding of human behaviour and the ability to develop open and honest relationships with the people to understand their abilities, concerns, interests and motivations.

Ability to inspire and motivate – Leadership requires line managers to be charismatic, highly organized, and very motivational in their interaction with the people. They develop a culture of hard work and commitment, inspiring and motivating the people to give their best to the organization.

Business understanding – Line managers with leadership qualities strive to have a clear understanding of their business, the environment in which they operate and their competitors. They develop an awareness of the strengths, weaknesses, opportunities and threats for their business and focus on maximizing resources to their full potential.

Managing organizational change – The role of a leader is crucial for managing organizational change, The process of organizational change is very complex and challenging and a competent and effective leadership is required to manage the situation.

Leadership determines excellent organizational performance. Leadership success in the implementation of the strategy is manifested in a conducive organizational climate, a reward strategy that is linked to strategic objectives, flexible structures that support business demands, and an effective organizational culture that influence behaviour in the right direction. The ultimate desired end results manifest itself in aligned individual and organizational performance.

LEADERSHIP PRINCIPLES FOR SUCCESS

There is no doubt that good project management is a critical factor of project success. That is, a project cannot be run without project management, be it formal or informal. You need to have something that holds things together. Underlying is the assumption that we need some form of order to organize and run a project. Someone has to do something. In this sense, project management helps set a frame, providing structure and order to potential chaos. Without this structure a project leads to nowhere; it will most likely fail, if it ever takes off.

If you want to generate results out of seemingly chaos you have to build structure that enables creativity, innovation, and results. Project management provides excellent tools to build this structure. They are important and necessary for project success. But are they sufficient? I don't think so. As a matter of fact, I claim that unless you gear them into the right direction, they remain ineffective. If you really want to secure project success you have to understand what it takes to set the right direction. Project management alone will not do the trick. What it takes is leadership - your leadership.

Without project leadership there is no direction in project management. Leadership is the decisive factor for improving the chances for projects to succeed. Consequently, effective project management needs to have a solid foundation based in project leadership. Without leadership, chances are that a project will be "just another project."

Based on my own experience in project management and the review of literature on leadership, project management, business, systems, and complexity theory I have identified five simple yet powerful leadership principles which, if applied systematically, can help you pave the path to project success.

The five leadership principles for project success are as follows:

Build vision

Nurture collaboration

Promote performance

Cultivate learning

Ensure results

Let's have a look at each principle one at a time.

P1: Build Vision

Sharing a common vision and goals and having the same understanding about tracking the progress towards this vision is one of the key factors in the success of a project and team.

Terry Sloan

A project vision sets the overall picture of your project. Project objectives qualify this vision, make it specific. Both project vision and project objectives are crucial for project success. Together they set the direction and tone of your project journey. They complement each other. The vision inspires your journey. It defines the purpose of your project.

The key to building vision is that people need to be able to relate to the vision in their daily activities. Give them the chance to identify themselves with the vision. Involve them in building this vision and participate in making it real. This helps build rapport and the necessary buy-in from those people to realize the project. Make them fans of the vision. Let it constitute their motivation and passion. Let them rave about it.

The story of a visitor who was curious about construction site illustrates the power of a common project vision. This visitor approached a group of workers to find out more about the construction. The first worker replied that he was a brick layer. The second worker told him that he was building a wall. Then he asked a third worker. This one explained that he and the other people in his team were building a cathedral. The interesting thing was that each worker was actually doing the same activity. Yet the motivations and their attitude differed a great deal. The third worker knew what he was devoting his time and effort to something big. His project may have been to build a wall. But it was the project vision of building a cathedral which enticed him.

A project vision without project objectives may give you an idea of the direction, but you may never get close enough to the destination to produce tangible results at a certain time. On the other hand, project objectives without a vision may describe the desired end result and time frame, but they cannot inspire the necessary enthusiasm in your team to drive the project to success. They do not form an underlying meaning for the work.

As a project leader you must make sure that both project vision and project objectives are in place. Project leaders do not start a project without a project vision and objectives. If you want to be or become a project leader, you either build vision and project objectives or make sure that both are in place, are crystal clear, and are mutually understood by every single person actively involved in the project. This is the meaning of the first leadership principle. Start with a unified vision and know where you stand before and during your project. Know your environment, know your potential, and identify your limits and overcome them. Build and involve your team and nurture effective collaboration across the board. This brings us to the second leadership principle: nurture collaboration.

P 2: Nurture Collaboration

A performing team yields synergy effects; the impossible becomes possible. This is why active team collaboration is crucial.

Project success is not about individual accomplishments. The project team delivers the project. As such, the team is the heart and soul of the project. Corollary, project success is, or at least should always be, the success of the team. Effective project leaders understand the value and huge potential of teamwork. This is why they actively nurture collaboration. They serve as role models and are part of the team. They thus actively participate and contribute to teamwork.

Collaboration is necessary for the team to achieve the vision and project objectives. By the same token, the project vision must include the concept of collaboration; it needs to be part of the vision as well as the project objectives. Collaboration is a means to achieve the objectives and thus to come closer to achieving the vision. It is a central element of every project. This is why vision and collaboration go hand in hand. You cannot move achieve project results without collaboration. On the other hand, collaboration without a common cause leads nowhere.

Collaboration is the juice of teamwork; it is what makes teamwork possible in the first place. It encompasses communication, individual and joint execution, as well as the delivery of results on both the individual and team level.

If you want to nurture collaboration you need to start with yourself. Be a role model to others: Share information openly. Give and accept open and constructive feedback. Be a good team player and work with your team.

Understand that the project is about the team. Project leadership becomes team leadership. It implies that if you want to be an effective project leader you have to be a good team player, too.

Nurturing collaboration can be hard at times. It takes a lot of effort and can be quite time consuming. The payoffs, however, are worth every minute invested. Having mutually understood and supported rules of engagement, characterized by open communication and effective collaboration, makes project life much easier. Once you have helped create an atmosphere of trust, team spirit, and fun, team synergy effects emerge. Magical things can happen, productivity increases, and the quality of the team's deliverables is higher. Nurturing collaboration prepares the ground for performance on the individual and team level. As a project leader you want to cultivate this soil of performance. This leads us to the third leadership principle: promoting performance.

P3: Promote Performance

Planning is good and important. At the end of the day you and your team have to perform. As a leader it is your responsibility to create an environment that promotes performance, on both the individual and team levels.

Building vision and nurturing collaboration are prerequisites for project success. Alas, they are useless if you cannot move your team to the performance stage. This is why you want to create an environment that helps promote performance.

The following rules help achieve this.

R1: Be a role model.

No matter what project you are working on, be aware that as project leader you are a role model to your own team and others. Act as such. Walk your own talk and be true to your own principles. Demonstrate authentic leadership.

R2: Create the right environment.

If you want to promote performance in your team, take the time and find out what motivates each individual team member and the team as a whole. Discover what the individual team members and the complete team need to perform. Learn how you can help the team perform.

R3: Empower your team.

You have to enable your team to do its job and perform. Give your team the power and all the information it needs to do its job and perform. Give your team the opportunity to excel and have an active hand in project success.

R4: Develop a solution-and-results orientation toward problems and risks.

Performing teams focus on solutions and results rather than problems. A problem or risk is not seen as a potential showstopper but a chance to learn and prove skills and competencies on the individual and group levels.

R5: Invite productive competition

Productive competitiveness can actually help promote performance - provided that the competitiveness aims at improving team performance and is linked with collaboration and social sharing.

R6: Let it happen

When you and your team have jointly built a common vision and developed collaboration rules, there should be no need to micromanage team members. Trust your team and let the team do its job.

Rule 7: Celebrate performance

Lasting performance can be achieved. It takes practice, training, endurance, and a results-driven attitude toward project challenges to develop and sustain it. Yet, performance and project success do not fall from heaven. You have to prepare and work for them, learning from mistakes and failures. There cannot be performance without training or learning. This leads us to the fourth leadership principle: cultivating learning.

P4: Cultivate Learning

As humans we all make mistakes. Effective leaders encourage their teams to explore new avenues and to make mistakes and learn from them. An effective leader builds in sufficient time for the team to learn, create, and innovate.

As project leader, you serve as partner and coach for learning and information sharing. You facilitate learning. You are not the sole source of information. Instead, create a learning environment in your team. Set the expectation that you want everyone in your team to join and support you in cultivating learning for the purpose of the project.

Learning is not a one-time activity, say, in the form of formal training prior or at the beginning of your project. It is ongoing and should become daily routine in your team. Establish regular sessions with your team where you review past performance, share information about planned accomplishments, address and resolve impediments together. Invite external reviews. Outside views offer different perspectives; fresh and unspoiled perspectives. If they aim to help the team identify formerly unknown risks and issues and overcome them, external project reviews can be a great learning opportunity.

When you or your team make mistakes, learn from them. Correct your shortcomings, improve your performance, and continue to work toward accomplishing the project vision. Cultivate learning from the beginning of your project. It significantly increases the speed at which your team can perform and sustain performance throughout and thus secure delivery.

Create room for your team members to be creative, to try something new, share their ideas, and learn from each other. Plan in sufficient time for your team to think outside the box, beyond the known path traveled, and to find new avenues to reach the goals of the projects. Empower your team to perform, make mistakes, learn, and innovate. This helps reduce uncertainty as information flows more freely. Team members are not afraid of making mistakes. They see mistakes as learning opportunities and they help each other solve problems. Corollary, if you want performance to yield the desired results you have to cultivate learning. There cannot be lasting performance without learning, and there cannot be results without performance.

P5: Ensure Results

Delivering results is both a prerequisite and an outcome of effective project leadership. Project delivery is a team effort, not an individual effort. The effective project leader builds and guides the team to deliver results by incorporating the first four leadership principles.

Ensuring results is not solely about end results. Neither is project success and project leadership. The fifth principle calls on us that in all our activities we keep the project vision in mind and produce results that benefit the purpose of the project. Project success is not defined by a single product or service delivered at the completion of a project. It is the accumulation of the many results yielded from each and every leadership principle. Vision, collaboration, performance, and learning are just as important. They culminate in results. When you talk about project success, the path to project results matters too. Corollary, an effective project leader always looks beyond the delivery of results.

The fifth principle of ensuring results reminds us that we have to make sure the results of the other four principles are aligned with the project vision and objectives. They have to serve the project purpose. Ensuring results is thus not an activity focusing only on the final project deliverables. It appeals to us that all of our project activities shall be results oriented, keeping the end deliverables in mind. It is a call for solution- and results-oriented leadership.

Ensuring results offer excellent learning opportunities, which in turn help boost collaboration, improve performance, give rise to innovation, and thus move us closer to realizing the project vision. Ongoing project results serve as a reflection of project leadership and how well the five leadership principles practiced. They reveal the true quality of team collaboration, team performance, and team learning. It is a form of quality assurance of effective project leadership for project success.

Dynamic Project Leadership

No single principle is the most important. It is the combination of all five leadership principles that helps secure project success. Building vision is the principle to start with, but you cannot achieve results if you do not embrace all five principles together as one system. Leadership is not merely the sum of applying the five principles.

It is understanding and living the dynamics within each principle as well as all five principles as a unit.

If you want to gain a deeper understanding of one particular leadership principle, you need to account for the remaining four principles and how they relate to the one you are looking at.

Applying the five leadership principles in daily project life requires the project leader to practice all five principles constantly and consistently. It is an ongoing exercise. Depending on where you are in a project, there may be a stronger emphasis on one or two principles. But you cannot isolate one from the others. Holistic leadership comprises all five principles.

CONCLUSION

Leadership is a process that requires buy-in, in order to

appropriately drive performance we must exhibit empathy with our expectations. Imagine a workplace where most of the heavy lifting is done by a select few in the absence of development and direction. Management spends most of its time meeting, conferencing, and analyzing reports without directly contributing to daily, weekly, or quarterly objectives. Belief, Ability, and Inspiration are artificial at best; those in position bathe in their Power instead of fueling purpose. This 'need to control' without contributing severs the binary alignment needed to optimize achievement. Leadership and its accountability directly reflect results and, subsequently, shoulder penalty as well as they do prize. Power is not Leadership, however, He who has the most Power, has the most responsibility, especially to Leadership. Try to be a Leader in our community and or society.

When assuming any new leadership roles there is one thing you can do to help pave the way for a succeful group dynastic. I call them the three promises. The key is to follow through on the promises. Don't just make them and then forget about them. Very close to your first day, either get everyone together for a meeting or send out a written form of this statement. If you make these promises and show your team that you mean them, you will have made a great start at becoming a very good Leader. Good luck.

1. I will never take credit for your accomplishments. Your hard work will be valued and recognized.
2. I will never publicly blame you for any mistake that happens. All mistakes are my fault. We may have a private discussion over how a situation should have been handled, however; all blame rest with me.
3. I will never separate from you in victory and I will never abandon you in defeat. We are in this together and we will rise or fall together.

www.ingramcontent.com/pod-product-compliance
Lightning Source LLC
Chambersburg PA
CBHW030728180526
45157CB00008BA/3095